A Muse Sings
A Swan Song

Mickey Wright

Morningwood Press | Dallas, GA

Mickey Wright/Morningwood Press
Box 2584
Dallas, GA 30132
www.amusesingsaswansong.com

Publisher's Note: This is a work of fiction. Names, characters, places, and incidents are a product of the author's imagination. Locales and public names are sometimes used for atmospheric purposes. Any resemblance to actual people, living or dead, or to businesses, companies, events, institutions, or locales is completely coincidental.

"Crocus" first appeared in Cricket; Mar2005, Vol. 32 Issue 7
"Flipped Rock" first appeared in The Heron's Nest;September 2013, Volume XV, Issue 3

Cover Artwork by Wayne Quackenbush

Logo by Sharon Williams

Book Layout Mickey Wright/BookDesignTemplates

A Muse Sings A Swan Song/ Mickey Wright. -- 1st ed.
ISBN 978-0-9990174-0-1

For when the muse's wings are spread air-ward,
who shall delay her flight?

–JOHN KEATS, HYPERION, A FRAGMENT

MICKEY WRIGHT

Contents

LIGHT

COME ON IN

Caution
Soul crossing
look both ways before

MICKEY WRIGHT

THE TROUBLE WITH MUSES

eeny meeny miny mo
once caught a muse up by her toe
but you know how the story goes
she left a heart filled up with poems

A WRINKLE IN TIME

Time has wrought runes
that my fingers lightly trace
upon your face
reading your story in Braille.
Cupping your chin
I learn from your eyes
you have become
world without end

FREEFALL

Eyes so blue to fall into
and fall
and fall
and fall.
And now I've fallen in so deep
I pray for each our souls to keep.
With each and every little death
and each and every catch of breath
and all the love we ever make
we'll build a bond that cannot break.
And if your tears should ever flow
I'll take each one and plant it so
that from each hurt a lotus grows.
The lotus blooms will one-by-one
open and reflect the sun
upon the we that now is one.

FORCE OF NATURE

I am the storm
that comes from the North
not unbidden
bleeding rain
to moisten
the earth
ready to
be plowed

You are the Earth
the mystery
the why
the woof
the warp
the weave
pattern
foundation

I am the Lightning
that quickens
brightly
lightly
the spark
that ignites
inflames
urges

You are the vein

[11]

the ore
the conductor
waving
the wind
billowing sails
the even keel
that sets course

We are the thunder
that rumbles
and echoes
from canyon
to tree
back and
forth
to home

RECURSION

Have we found each other before?
Perhaps as souls traveling
between there and here?
Are we entwined in forever
finding each other
again and again
reveling
in our joy
loving then dying?
Do we lose us to the darkness?
Do we find us in the darkness
or must we wait to be reborn?
First forgetting,
then struggling again
through life
through other lovers
learning
growing
preparing
without even knowing why
until we find us again

MICKEY WRIGHT

and it all becomes clear
Forever begins now as it has before -
à jamais commence maintenant
let us rejoice
let us live
every precious moment,
but never as the last.

INEFFABLE

You can't see it
but like the wind you feel it
reflected
from another's eyes
a reflection of you.
And when you do
like a typhoon, tsunami or tornado
you are swept away
helplessly,
y no hay remedio.
And even if there were
you would refuse it.
The moon, the magnet, the maelstrom
inexorable
implacable
inescapable
remember Tantalus and Sisyphus.

MICKEY WRIGHT

MAELSTROM

On an empty sea
gentle waves open
and engulf me in a swirling maelstrom.
        -Who
Spinning
        -Am
Dizzy
        -I
Down
        -Now?
soft slippery slopes.
Deeper and deeper
I-me-who? plummets drowning
In the sweetness.
Beguiled
by the essence
that envelops.
And the more of me that
is lost
the more of me
I see.
And the me
and the not me
swirl, dancing
within the maelstrom
seeking

precious release
that comes
with joyful
Singularity.

AUTUMN

In autumn,
second hand hearts love
like it's their first
when it could be their last
if they are lucky
enough to have learned
the bittersweet lessons
from the ghosts of seasons past.
Contused memories.
Blemished records.
Wounds and scars.
Loss and regret
gathered like fruit in a basket.
Peel them even though
they are way past ripe.
Divine from the seeds
and tracery of veins.
Discard the pith,
but heed the pulp
sweet or bitter.

CATARACT

Heat
Like forest fire flames
Rushing through the pines
Comes over me

Tresses tickle my shoulders
Lips brush
Eyes aglitter
Souls rise together
Seeking
Finding
Rushing
Over the precipice

To cascade down
The cataract
Into a peaceful pool
Floating

Water nearly still
Breathing calms
Heartbeats slow
But never diminish.

INNER ANGEL

we all have angels
inside us
but
until we let them out
give them to another
they are trapped
caged
within our hearts
wanting only
to be set free
do angels trapped
for too long
become our demons?

MUSIC OF THE SPHERES

Do you hear the music of the spheres
in the drop of dew from a leaf?
The drip from an icicle?
In the rumble of coming thunder?
In the moan of the dove,
whisperer of your soul's soul?

MICKEY WRIGHT

BATTERED HEARTS

battered hearts-
afraid
to take chances
longing for what
always seems just out of reach.
can they find the other
who is longing
hiding
cautious
timorous-trembling
but wanting?
the spark, sharp
shoots the gap -
electric sighs
a dance
to dare
to care

FRAGILE

imagine the wonder of a butterfly held
cupped in the hands of a small child.
imagine the delight, the sheer joy,
the responsibility
the child
has
at holding this small piece of the universe,
this small life, fluttery, colorful
fragile, easily crushed
but nonetheless –
life.
Now imagine my heart, my soul
held in your sweet hands
fluttery, fragile
easily crushed
but nonetheless –
safe.

MICKEY WRIGHT

LOVE'S GRAVITY

In a radial parabolic trajectory
the relative velocity
of the two objects
is always the escape velocity
There are two cases:
the bodies move away from each other
or towards each other.

SIMPLE PLEASURES

raking leaves I watch your face
raking leaves I drink you in
raking leaves the sun warms us in shared rays
raking leaves your quiet strength
raking leaves your voice a song
raking leaves - simple sweet
-as we share time
raking leaves we form a bond
raking leaves we come together
completion

EPHEMERA

For just a day
the mayfly
lives,
loves,
begets.
In hubris only
is love
sure
to last
forever.

SATURNALIA

What whispers Winter to the Spring
preparing it for living things
set to come and bare their fruits
once covered by their daily suits

All poised and set to show their best;
lift themselves above the rest
to find the love they know awaits
to blunder forth and procreate

To fill the forest, hill and vale
with kith and kin - the holy grail
filled with madness, joy and glee
forever wild, always free

To eat and drink the bounty set
by nature's nurture to beget
and in the moonlight, dance and sing
'til from the stones their voices ring

Fires rise and heat the dawn
exhausted bodies on the lawn
twitching spasms gasp for breath
stolen by their little deaths

MICKEY WRIGHT

Drunk on love, lust and joy
past the point of needed ploy
fields to plow, seeds to plant
passing on what life will grant.

SOULMATES

moving within
the other
one
of the
one become two -
on this mundane plane.
trying madly to
remerge.
re-emerge
reaching for heaven-
for satori without nirvana.
not yet ready
to give up
the essence.
still moving-
closer-
closer-
I gasp-
almost-
then…

MICKEY WRIGHT

the one
sadly returns to two,
the joy
being too great
to bear
for now.

Mmmmm

languid velvet love
whispered breeze
cools my seared skin

MICKEY WRIGHT

EVERYTHING

the universe encircled
in my arms
I hold tightly

FOR CRIMSON

Soft whicker from the barn as I enter
scents of straw, manure and leather
The horsey smell of her face
the essence of this place
puffs of warm breath and eyes
go wide and roll in surprise
at this forward-eyed predator
that cares for her.

MICKEY WRIGHT

To KACY

Her tail thumped the blanketed
floor.
Her faith and trust shook me to the
core.
I whispered through
tears
as I heard her breathing
slow
and with my hand on her
heart
I felt both
stop
as she ran through the field
of my
mind.
I still have her
collar.

TO THE MAIDEN

To the maiden
retreated to her
ivory tower
locking
the door
burning
the ladder
behind:
Towers can be
cloisters
redoubts
talismans
against pain
but not even
gargoyles
can repel
the demons of
feeling forever.
Princess
let down your hair
so one who
cares,
the knight
in tarnished armor
may ascend,

MICKEY WRIGHT

breach
the fortress
crumble the wall
and protect your heart
Toujours.

PSALM OF MY HEART

I hold you
in the psalm
of my heart

Dear

A place no one has
been before
A place prepared
by the fires of desire
that cooled to embers
having never reached
this hallowed
chamber of my soul
reserved by God
for someday

now

You appear on

MICKEY WRIGHT

soft angel wings
that flutter
in my chest
every time
I look at you

I know
exultation

SECOND CHANCES

I passed this
exit once before
during a storm
and though it looked
to be a beautiful place
with peace and love
the rain blurred my vision
and I drove past.
The heart of the storm,
the tempest,
tossed me about
and injured, I lost
time from my journey.
But I am a lucky man.
I live a charmed life.
So I took the chance
when allowed.
I steered into the exit
and found the paradise
I had passed by.
The sun portends
a future full of light

MICKEY WRIGHT

and though none of us
can know,
this road seems clear.

SOCKS IN THE DRYER

love,
like the lost sock
from the dryer.
you think it gone
for good
then one day
it reappears
dusty and covered with lint.
is the mate still in the drawer?

MICKEY WRIGHT

ABSENCE

the empty space beside me
has presence.
I reach for you
and find only sheets.
my kiss goes
unanswered.
my arm seeks
and finds only
memory.
soonest is not soon
enough.

IN ANY LANGUAGE

EN FRANÇAISE

La forêt est profonde, sombre
Et plein d'arbres
Je vois beaucoup de lumières au-delà
Beaucoup attirent
Mais un seul se distingue
toi, mon amour

EN ANGLAISE

The forest is deep, dark
and full of trees
I see many lights beyond
they beckon
but only one stands out
you, my love

[43]

BATH

Hot water, steam rising
Redolent of lavender and lemons
Languissant toes meet mine and mingle
Delight to the touch
Cherished treasures of time
Precious sensuous
A smile
That sears my soul

BEGINNING OF THE END

O moan
the shiny coin
tarnished.

What shone like the dawn's sun
has changed
a shadow has crossed

But the coin is gold
it's value
intrinsic

still legal tender
and still beautiful
still valuable

I keep it in
my breast pocket
close

🦋 DARK 🦋

SHADOWS

When the long shadows come creeping out
and you find that
the cobwebs hid
more than spiders
then what is one to do?
Brooms for spiders
but the shadows
oh the shadows.
Brooms can't sweep them away.
Cardboard won't contain them.
Photos won't drive them off.
Can I tuck them in the back of my mind
or will they just play there
leaving treacherous footprints?
Paths to follow
and better not to stray.
Keep off the grass.
Beware the webs.

EXILE

We wait
in the hills above my village.
The full moon bathes us -
bright enough to cast
shadows sharp as the knives
we each carry at our side,
whetted on sandstone.
I lick my lips.

Cast out three years before
I have made my way back
through jungle and ice floe
mountain and shire and
fields of somnambulent poppies
that bade me stop and smell
and rest
and delay.

I can see below the house of elders,
uncles no doubt squatting
in idiotic contentment,
secure in their contempt,

as their reed walls decay
to a powdery dust
that protects them no more
than their brains.

We-
the gathered and I,
paint ourselves with
yolk and soaked rich red
earth crumbled from
clay we mine from the
fossilized bank
of a long dead stream.

Where did they come from,
these gathered?
How did they know to find me
here?
Did I leave a spoor?
Did they sniff me out?
And if so, does a pure scent
mean my advent is righteous?

Bats and nightjars fill
the air overhead-
strobing, moon borne shadows.

MICKEY WRIGHT

Wheeling like starlings
they fume and feint
villageward.
My brothers of the night sky-
who among you shall return alive?

The gathered dance naked
around the flayed carcass of
a cow cut from a herd not theirs.
With no fire to light
their movements or cook with
they will eat the meat
cold and bloody.
A sacrament

I will not eat until
my rightful place
has been secured
and the table of my
ancestors
has been set with the
platters, cutlery and tankards
of my bride.

I will not sleep
I will not rest
I will not stop

Until -
my vengeance complete,
my legacy restored,
peace and balance
reign again.

ALCHEMY

Drunk as a skunk
the drunk monk
drank from a
mug of lead.

White powder
dusted his fingers
and sowed his brain
with erosion.
Corrosion of
ambrosia lost him
the angels
and seraphs,

and conferred
no immortality
but cost him thought
and mobility

.STORM SHIP

Rise and fall
rise and fall.
Waves crash over the bow
that forges into the tempest.
Petrels wheel.
Beware the following sea!

ANNIHILATION

What does one do
when a heart is returned
sliced
diced
and served up
on a silver platter?
When the crow
is a pile of
feathers
and you can eat no more?
Could you stuff
the hole in your chest
with the feathers
and seal it with the platter?
Or will the feathers flutter
in the breeze that blows
through the hollow
like the wind
through the pines
that soughs a song
lonely and bereft?

REARVIEW

The rearview mirror is filled with faces
and the road behind
with scattered ashes
blowing in the wind
swirling motes, galaxies of gone.
Tearing the mirror away
I throw it out the window
but even with the faces gone -
urgent whispers
lost caresses
faded feel of lips on my nape
friends and lovers lost
like tears in rain
washed away like sins
that aren't sins
and as they dwindle
they wave, and
I lift my hand.

MY CHILD MIND

The child's hand in mine
the child's mind
behind mine.
My tuatara eye opens
lidless
mindless
all seeing
but not believing
encompassing my being
and now I'm believing
however fleeting
that the dawn
is chasing me
to the cliff.
Buffalo jump
one big lump
bump of blood brain and bone
You cannot go home
and so my mind roams
tossed by waves of
sea green foam.
What's going on
with halcyon?
What's going on?
Where's halcyon?
The hand in mine

fresh from
the coal mine
sifts black dust
so fine
it coats my mind
my child's mind.

MICKEY WRIGHT
SWAN SONG

He stalked it through forests
green with leaves while birds trilled
and whistled sweet melodies.

He hunted it in the mountains
tall gray and wreathed in mist
while glaciers clashed live cymbals.

Over the plains he tried to
run it down like the cheetah
the grass whispering against his legs.

On the reefs he used a steel trident
in the coralaceous crannies as
dolphins and whales cried all around.

Dogs pulled his sled across the frozen
arctic wastes howling along with the wind
that built great drifts in his path.

In the great desert he carried water
in ostrich eggs emptied and plundered
while hyenas chuckled softly at his folly.

He went to the ends of the earth
and back again,
but it stayed one step ahead
or he was always one step behind.

Finally one day he cornered it
in the back of a dark city alley and
with the slash of an axe
he killed the song.

With the deed done
the song within himself died.
and he died with it.

MICKEY WRIGHT

DREAM

A shadow chases me
there is no escape
it lopes right along
a hard knuckled ape.
I turn, dodge and run
smack dab into it
just out of reach
out at the limits.
The days that are cloudy
I search high and low
but the next time I see it
is in the moon's glow.

MONUMENT

Stand beneath the cliff
and watch the water drip
down the face
spreading algal stains
on darkened shale.
Impassive, massive, edifice
the tears belie the artifice
of the eyes
whose loss of care
shadow noon light.
Fractures in the fair visage
create a glossy clipped montage
of bits and parts
like nose and lips
and chicane grin.
Suddenly its all acrumble
-falls apart to scattered rubble
pieces tumbled
far and near
no one to pick them up.

MICKEY WRIGHT
DOGMA

The war was won
the fighting done
ants picked the carcass clean

From high above
a thorny dove
flew in on razor wings

It's haloed head
filled all with dread
who stayed that charnel field

It's lidless eyes
looked, surmised
was nothing left to do

With time to kill
and blood to spill
it headed once more west

Toward fields of green
not yet turned mean
where living things still grow

To share the words
they've not yet heard.
To spread it's vicious lies

So watch on high.
and shade your eyes.
Be prepared to run

Because this dove
takes all you love
and leaves you dead and cold

TIME

The beast at my back
breathes down my neck
fangs slavering
dripping corrosion
eroding the hands
that tell the time.
Do I need them to tell?
Does not the setting sun
reflect the horizon behind
that is always out of reach
but never out of touch?
Dear and sweet and lost,
grains of sand taken
by the undertow.
Which wave will be the last?

INBETWEEN

CHOICES

When it came time
To decide upon a career
I had two choices
Carpenter or poet
I chose poet
because in poetry
The corners
Don't have to meet
As long as the door still opens

MICKEY WRIGHT

SENSES OF COMMON REALITY

Do you hear the rainbow in a dragonfly wing?
Or the sky from the back of the kingfisher?
Can you taste the wind in a blade of grass
or the heat in a meteor trail?
Can you smell yellow in dappled sunlight
or blue from a summer storm?
Do snowflakes hum and buzz in your ear
or a sunset tickle your shoulders?
Dance I say. Dance.
Raise up your arms.
Throw out your hands
Fling your voice against the mountain
and return next week for its echo.
Drum the dark hollow,
for who sets convention
but us?
Who filters the senses
and makes sense of them?
Tucks them into neat cubbies with
squid ink letters on burdock labels
but us?
We make real the unreal and call it essential.
Wear it on our wrists
and pressed against our ears

.

We wrench darkness from the light
- Reverse Genesis -
and from the scattered atoms
new ashes arise,
new toys for our brains to flay,
our hearts to wrap around
and misunderstand.
So that on a bruised day dawning
under a swollen, gravid moon
our tribe might rise again.

LIFE

Swirling up in rising ringlets
campfire smoke from
crackled logs
smell of the dawn of man
and the kettle at dawn
has not yet whistled
but the steam from it's pout
circles the smoke
chasing
playing
as dawn dawns I yawn
and looking
up see hawks
a kettle
and all the swirling
all the helices
and all that I can see
are kettles and smoke and steam
rife life fire
and the dance
neverending

.

LOSS OF AWE AND WONDER

The dimples
under your shoulder blades
are the scars
from where your wings once fit.
Where have they gone?
No one can
take them from you-
belief
is the glue that
held them in place.
When we lose
"once upon a time"
and
"step on a crack"
our wings
fly away
fly away
fly away gone.

CREATIVITY

From within a cloister
of my choosing
hot sauce
from an oyster
oozing
thoughts, ideas –
a brain in flames
fevered pitch

RENDEZVOUS

Sunlight cascading
through skeletal branches
of leaf barren trees
seduces rainbows
from the ice
beading the gaunt fingers.
Colors so pure it makes me ache.

I walk down the path of my past
toward reconciliation if not redemption,
following a ramshackle stone wall,
a neglected remnant of time déshabillé,
whose flat fossil-filled shale
once patiently piled
one atop another
now fall down in places:
pitiful piles of rubble.

I meander to the bottom
where the morass roils,
shrouded from the sun
by cerements of aromatic cedars.
Without the sun

MICKEY WRIGHT

it has become
too dark
to explore today.
Perhaps tomorrow?

DAMAGED ONE

which one of us
 is the damaged one?
 or are we all?
 or of all of us, are none?

MICKEY WRIGHT

HARDWARE

The flypaper lost its stickiness
after years of dirt and dust and mess.
Still the window sill is filled
with the husks of many long past killed.

The buzzing flies still pestering
the old gold battered lettering
cannot read the faded lines
of this decrepit Hardware sign.

Still abrim with nuts and nails
expensive things in gilded jails
hammers, saws and power tools
and of course, a few loose screws.

Everything I'll need aquire
all my crafty heart's desires
can still be found deep within
these old decrepit, bygone bins

All the wisdom. All the saws.
All the maxims ever was,
are on display for one to buy
though the prices are so high.

Still the cost must be borne
for aphorisms that shopworn
so that someday I might see
a thornless Monkey Puzzle tree.

MICKEY WRIGHT

WILL THE SUN STILL RISE?

Will the sun still rise?
The cock still crow?
Will the tides still change;
the ebb and flow?
Will streams still run?
Blood still be red?
Or will all be gone
when I am dead?
Is all the future
Naught but past?
Twas there nothing done
That were done to last?
Will the last just stop
and turn to dust?
Or will my blood
turn to rust?

WORDS

Words are minded things
and on their own
can run wild
on the table.
Rack them up
shoot the cue…
break
but they won't go neatly
into pockets.
They bump and bank and spin
and align in ways not tended.
Call the shot but –
angles are everything.
And when the score
is tallied
You can lose by winning.

CROCUS

An abstract painting in the round
Lies nestled in the frozen ground.
A purple palette packed just so
Then whitewashed by the winter's snow
'Til sun and rain seep through the soil
And leaves and roots begin their toil
Of sending shoots to seek the light
Then bursting forth in sheer delight
Of blossom-colored morning dew

Proclaiming spring is born anew.

COURAGE

Deer gather at the edge of the woods
one foot in one world
one in another.
Skittish
The best grass grows out in the open
but the risk is high.
Dark things lurk in the long grass.
unseen
unknown
Nervously they prance
heads held high, nostrils wide
tails nervous, twitching
ready to raise the flag.
Who among them has the temerity
to take that first step?

MICKEY WRIGHT

DUST

that starlight traveled
billions of light years
to shine on you and me
so who are we
to waste it?

ATTENDENT

sitting in a tattered wicker chair
in the anteroom of the restroom
his mop and bucket and cleaners at the ready
listening to the basest voices
all day long
he nodded as I left
and I wondered what he talked about
when he went home

MICKEY WRIGHT

THE RISE OF SOCIAL MEDIA

The moon moves through my solitude.
Fundy tides pull me
toward thoughts I had long since banished
and sent away on whippoorwill wings
through boughs of mistletoe.

The lightning strikes
and fulgurites
form in the sands of my time -
beaches branching into rivulets and deltas
effluent, affluent - treasures run to the sea.

The stuff of legends.
Legends in their own minds
flee the carnage and chaos for greener fields,
pastures for poseurs, mast for mediocre mimes.
Marceu rolls over in his imaginary box

Who are these "gods"
these "Titans" who walk the digital planes
filling my laptop with their patent homilies?
nuggets of nothing that pass as philosophy.
What rough beast indeed!

ALPHABET SOUP

In this climate
Of heated political correctness
I think
that instead
Of Alphabet soup
We should have
Alphanumeric soup
With a few radicals
And irrational numbers
Thrown in.
And from our square roots
Maybe we can
Burn our Algebras
To free up
The binaries
And fire up a few
Prime numbers

MODERN FAMILY

With apologies and thanks to Mr. Frost

Crammed with fillers, fats and oils
Fast food wrapped in golden foil
The kids don't know the 'rents don't care
As long as they all get their share

They take their places grab a seat
where each can see and hear and eat.
The great and highly powered screen
Demand attention sharp and keen

Ads for weight loss, drugs and loans
Computer games and cars and drones
It's really quite a revelation
so much more than conversation

And though no dinner bell did ring
They really have to watch this thing
And other shows before they sleep
And other shows before they sleep

[88]

TOY CHEST

my child within's room
acclutter
strewn with discarded
toys
"put them away or
I'll throw it all out."
only wish that I could

KISMET

Sunrise over the desert
Dry water colors
On paintbrush sage
Owl peers from a saguaro hole
Watching the pack rat
Hide a bauble in its den
Not knowing how close
It was
To
The sky

JUST REWARDS

We are all into this river born
And like salmon
We swim toward home
Against the current
Only to stack up against
The dam of gold
That blocks our souls
From the ladder dreamt of.
Rail against the gleam
Forsake the dragon's hoard
And the rungs will be revealed
And lead you to the light.

CONNECTIONS

connections
like potholders woven
by spiders on acid
the pastiche of our lives
warp and woof altered
to fit today
forward
refresh-reset the dawn

ALTERATIONS

"No left turn shall be unstoned"
 the prankster cried with glee
then leapt up high in to the air
and felt that he was free
The prankster was not up there long
before he tumbled down
he could not figure what went wrong
before he hit the ground

MICKEY WRIGHT

UNREQUITED

I am the leaf
tattered and thin
wet and stuck
to a riverbed stone.
organic on inorganic
clinging to the slippery
algal immoveable rock.
cold and stolid
stuck in place
collecting the debris
so prized that it allows
the river to flow by
without taking even a sip

eventually the leaf falls away
the rock still
like a waterwheel
spinning in place
over and over
unchanging

OBLIVIOUS

Steam rises from
each droplet
on the pavement-
the tropics
in a teacup.
The treefrog nestles
snug behind the hanging art
content in hiding
its sublime beauty
from prying eyes
and its eggs
from lascivious attentions
predatory intentions.
How many wander through life
not lost
but short of sight
blind to beauty?

MICKEY WRIGHT

THE UNEXAMINED LIFE

I was not there.
I turned 'round quickly
but still not there.
No spark,
no flash,
no filling of empty air
to say
I had been.
I know that I had felt
myself creeping up behind me
avec mauvais intentions
perhaps to pickpocket my dreams.
None he less
I was not there.

❦ NOT SO HIGH COOs ❦

sultry night
answer from the shadows
Katy did

a chipped vase
a quiet rainy day
nascence

MICKEY WRIGHT

your soul flies by
on soft sad-silent wings
and whippoorwill cries

spreading warmth
the fire contained
within the hearth

I never told her.
Regrets reflected
by taillights in rain.

barcode
sunlight through the deck slats

MICKEY WRIGHT

crop circles
yellow
beneath the plant pots

still pond
daughter's face over mine
ripples spoil our likeness

swaying pines
the needles
softly sough sighs

Pitted penny facedown
in a handicap spot
were you ever spent on a thought?

MICKEY WRIGHT

Snow, like bird splat
crusts the mountains
surrounding Las Vegas

if there were no clouds
how would we ever know
the depth of the blue

chilly wave
foam fingers
chase the piping plovers south

crumpled papers on the floor
orphaned words
gather in pools of thought

MICKEY WRIGHT

median guardrail
single grass stalk
shades the pavement

far star's light
I think it might
be the dust of me

cradle in a bough
two pearls
hold everything

does lightning know
what thunder says
through the rain's static?

MICKEY WRIGHT

indiscriminate
the swirling mists veil
and quiet the cry of the crow

frost flower glitters
reflecting diamonds back
to the sun that kills it

shadows flutter down
motes on sunny ground
rise to meet landing sparrows

green glints
remnants of yesterday's fun
shattered

MICKEY WRIGHT

Mother Nature
saw her children spill
jonquil tears

fractal forkings
meander on maple leaves
lifeblood of waffles

flipped rock
scurry of vivid colors

white birches
runes against the snow
she remembers me today

MICKEY WRIGHT

pup worries
the worn leather collar
is still too large

warm January day
out of time
a lizard basks on a rock

glimmer of an idea
trout chases minnows
into sunlight

ephemera
fallen flowers and mayflies
float past the head stones

MICKEY WRIGHT

angry words
swarming bees
can't return to the hive

in retrospect
no wait
I never

Full moon whispered
porch light whimsies eclipse your lips

INDEX TO TITLES
AND FIRST LINES

A

B

C

I

J

K

L

M

T

U

W

Y

MICKEY WRIGHT

About the Author

"Making poetry accessible and enjoyable to everyone. " That's Mickey's motto. Poetry has dropped out of favor as an art form in recent years and Mickey's mission is to revive it by writing verse that is not only intricately layered and crafted to appeal to any literati, but is also easily readable and enjoyable by anyone of any level of literary experience.

Professional skier, zookeeper, teacher, prison guard, ecologist, wildlife manager, life safety consultant, Mickey has had a lifetime of experiences that has built the inner world that he shares in his writing. This world comes to life and is populated by new ideas and new images that burst from the page.

Love, loss, pain and exultation are all part of his poems along with nature, beauty and the environment.

Come on in. Experience the universe in a new and unique way.

MICKEY WRIGHT

MICKEY'S FORTHCOMING NOVEL, "TOXIC
LOVE" WILL BE AVAILABLE IN EARLY 2018

Morningwood Press | Dallas, GA

NOTES

Morningwood Press | Dallas, GA

MICKEY WRIGHT

NOTES

Morningwood Press | Dallas, GA

NOTES

Morningwood Press | Dallas, GA

MICKEY WRIGHT

NOTES

Morningwood Press | Dallas, GA

NOTES

Morningwood Press | Dallas, GA